The Pied of Hamelin

by Robert Browning
abridged by Christine Hall and Martin Coles

Setting the scene

The legend of the Pied Piper is about something that happened in Hamelin in Germany between 700 and 800 years ago. No one knows exactly what happened, but there have been stories about it ever since!

Robert Browning wrote his poem about the Pied Piper in 1849 when his son was born. He based his poem on a German legend. Since that time, Robert Browning's poem has become the most famous English version of this well-known German story.

Hamelin Town's in Brunswick,
By famous Hanover city;
The river Weser, deep and wide,
Washes its wall on the southern side;
A pleasanter spot you never spied;
But, when begins my ditty,
Almost five hundred years ago,
To see the townsfolk suffer so
From vermin, was a pity.

spied saw
ditty poem
vermin pests

The Pied Piper

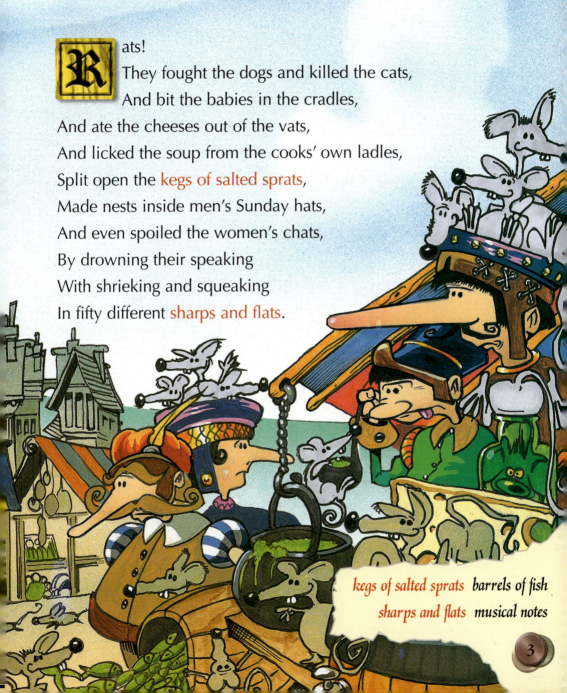

Rats!
They fought the dogs and killed the cats,
And bit the babies in the cradles,
And ate the cheeses out of the vats,
And licked the soup from the cooks' own ladles,
Split open the kegs of salted sprats,
Made nests inside men's Sunday hats,
And even spoiled the women's chats,
By drowning their speaking
With shrieking and squeaking
In fifty different sharps and flats.

kegs of salted sprats barrels of fish
sharps and flats musical notes

At last the people in a body
To the Town Hall came flocking:
"'Tis clear," cried they, "our Mayor's a noddy;
And as for our Corporation – shocking! ...
Rouse up, sirs! Give your brains a racking
To find the remedy we're lacking,
Or, sure as fate, we'll send you packing!"
... At this the Mayor and Corporation
Quaked with a mighty consternation.

remedy cure
consternation worry

The Pied Piper

An hour they sat in council,
    At length the Mayor broke silence …
    "It's easy to bid one rack one's brain –
I'm sure my poor head aches again,
I've scratched it so, and all in vain
Oh for a trap, a trap, a trap!"
Just as he said this, what should hap
At the chamber door but a gentle tap?
"Bless us," cried the Mayor, "what's that?
… Only a scraping of shoes on the mat?
Anything like the sound of a rat
Makes my heart go pit-a-pat!"

rack one's brains **think hard**

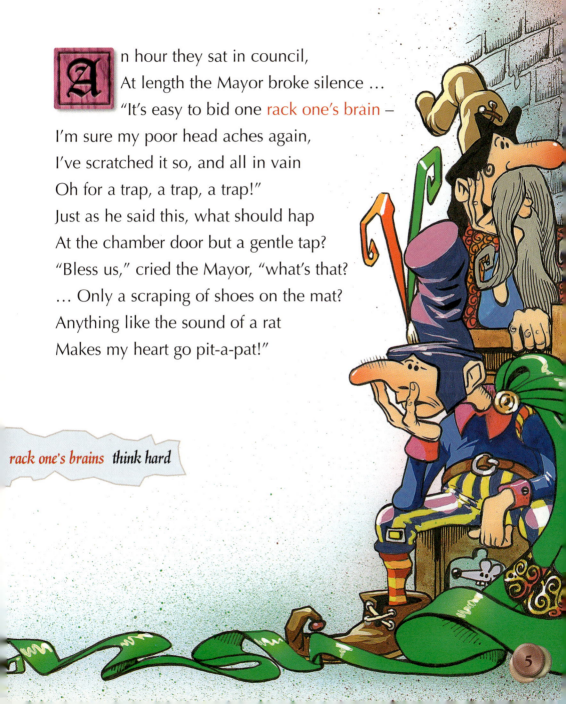

"Come in!" – the Mayor cried, looking bigger:
And in did come the strangest figure!
His queer long coat from heel to head
Was half of yellow and half of red,
And he himself was tall and thin,
With sharp blue eyes, each like a pin …

The Pied Piper

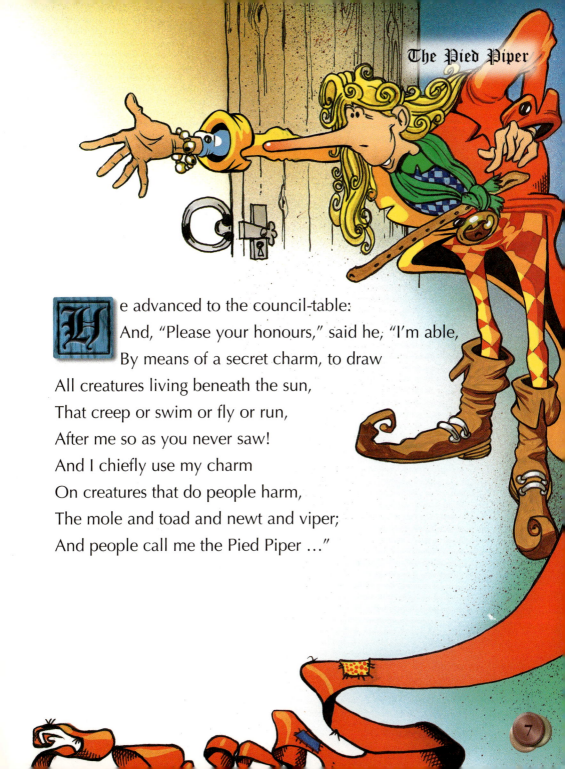

He advanced to the council-table:
And, "Please your honours," said he, "I'm able,
By means of a secret charm, to draw
All creatures living beneath the sun,
That creep or swim or fly or run,
After me so as you never saw!
And I chiefly use my charm
On creatures that do people harm,
The mole and toad and newt and viper;
And people call me the Pied Piper …"

"And as for what your brain bewilders,
If I can rid your town of rats
Will you give me a thousand guilders?"
"One? fifty thousand!" – was the exclamation
Of the astonished Mayor and Corporation.

bewilders is confused about
guilders gold coins

The Pied Piper

Into the street the Piper stept,
   Smiling first a little smile,
   As if he knew what magic slept
In his quiet pipe the while;
Then, like a musical adept,
To blow the pipe his lips he wrinkled,
And green and blue his sharp eyes twinkled,
Like a candle-flame where salt is sprinkled;
And ere three shrill notes the pipe uttered,
You heard as if an army muttered;
And the muttering grew to a grumbling;
And the grumbling grew to a mighty rumbling …

adept expert
ere before

And out of the houses the rats came tumbling.
Great rats, small rats, lean rats, brawny rats,
Brown rats, black rats, grey rats, tawny rats,
Grave old plodders, gay young friskers,
Fathers, mothers, uncles, cousins,
Cocking tails and pricking whiskers,
Families by tens and dozens,
Brothers, sisters, husbands, wives –
Followed the Piper for their lives.
From street to street he piped advancing,
And step for step they followed dancing,
Until they came to the river Weser
Wherein all plunged and perished!

plunged dived
perished died

You should have heard the Hamelin people
Ringing the bells till they rocked the steeple
"Go," cried the Mayor, "and get long poles,
Poke out the nests and block up the holes!
Consult with carpenters and builders,
And leave in our town not even a trace
Of the rats!" – when suddenly, up the face
Of the Piper perked in the market-place,
With a, "First, if you please, my thousand guilders!"

The Pied Piper

A thousand guilders! The Mayor looked blue;
So did the Corporation too …
To pay this sum to a wandering fellow
With a gipsy coat of red and yellow!
"Beside," quoth the Mayor with a knowing wink,
"Our business was done at the river's brink;
We saw with our eyes the vermin sink,
And what's dead can't come to life, I think …
But as for the guilders, what we spoke
Of them, as you very well know, was in joke.
Beside, our losses have made us thrifty.
A thousand guilders! Come, take fifty!"

> quoth said
> thrifty careful

The Piper's face fell, and he cried,
"No trifling! I can't wait, beside!
... And folks who put me in a passion
May find me pipe after another fashion."

The Pied Piper

"ou threaten us, fellow? Do your worst,
Blow your pipe there till you burst!"

Once more he stept into the street,
And to his lips again
Laid his long pipe of smooth straight cane …
There was a rustling that seemed like a bustling
Of merry crowds justling at pitching and hustling,
Small feet were pattering, wooden shoes clattering,
Little hands clapping and little tongues chattering,
And, like fowls in a farm-yard when barley is scattering,
Out came the children running.
All the little boys and girls,
With rosy cheeks and flaxen curls,
And sparkling eyes and teeth like pearls,
Tripping and skipping, ran merrily after
The wonderful music with shouting and laughter.

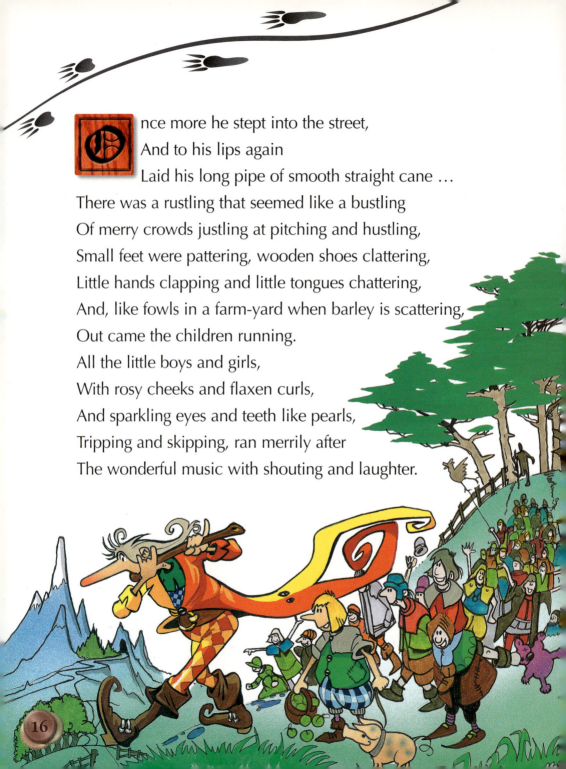

The Pied Piper

The Mayor was dumb, and the Council stood
As if they were changed into blocks of wood,
Unable to move a step, or cry
To the children merrily skipping by,
– Could only follow with the eye
That joyous crowd at the Piper's back …
When, lo, as they reached the mountain-side,
A wondrous portal opened wide,
As if a cavern was suddenly hollowed;
And the Piper advanced and the children followed,
And when all were in to the very last,
The door in the mountain-side shut fast.

portal door

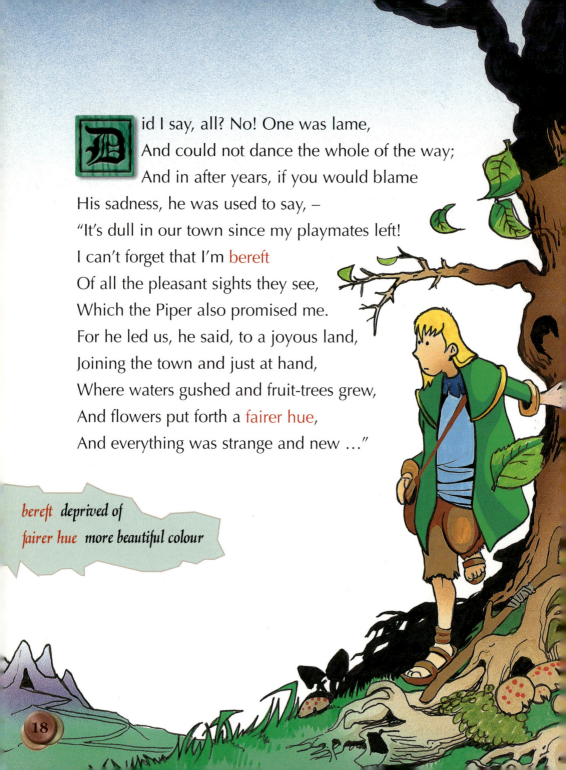

Did I say, all? No! One was lame,
And could not dance the whole of the way;
And in after years, if you would blame
His sadness, he was used to say, –
"It's dull in our town since my playmates left!
I can't forget that I'm bereft
Of all the pleasant sights they see,
Which the Piper also promised me.
For he led us, he said, to a joyous land,
Joining the town and just at hand,
Where waters gushed and fruit-trees grew,
And flowers put forth a fairer hue,
And everything was strange and new …"

bereft *deprived of*
fairer hue *more beautiful colour*

The Pied Piper

Alas, alas for Hamelin!
… The mayor sent East, West, North and South,
To offer the Piper, by word of mouth,
Wherever it was men's lot to find him,
Silver and gold to his heart's content,
If he'd only return the way he went,
And bring the children behind him.

And the better in memory to fix
The place of the children's last retreat,
They called it, the Pied Piper's Street …
But opposite the place of the cavern
They wrote the story on a column,
And on the great church-window painted
The same, to make the world acquainted
How their children were stolen away,
And there it stands to this very day.

acquainted aware

So, Willy, let me and you be wipers
　　Of scores out with all men – especially pipers!
And, whether they pipe us free from rats or from mice,
If we've promised them *aught*, let us keep our promise!

aught anything

Looking back

Pages 2 and 3
The town of Hamelin has a terrible problem with rats.

Pages 4 and 5
The Mayor and town council do not know how to deal with the problem.

Pages 6 and 7
The Pied Piper says he can solve the problem of the rats.

Pages 8 and 9
The Mayor agrees to pay the Pied Piper 1000 guilders.

Pages 10 and 11
The Pied Piper charms the rats from the houses and they drown in the river.

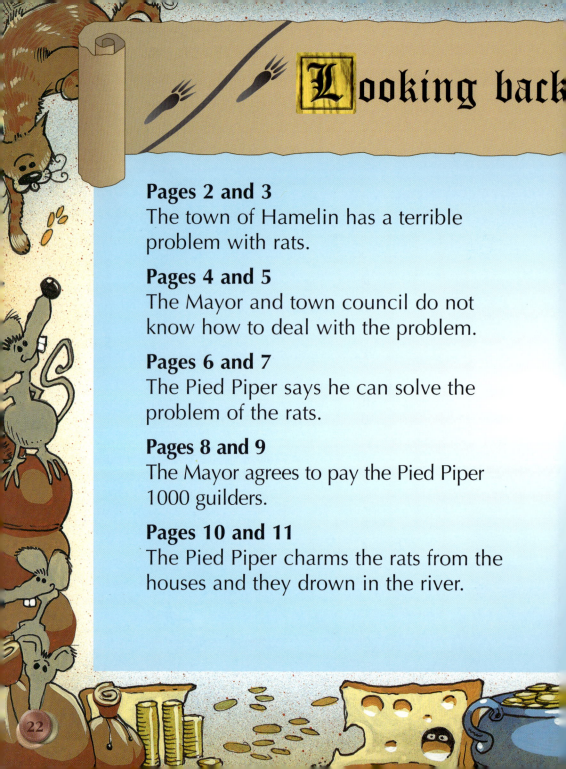

on the story

Pages 12 and 13
The people are happy but the Mayor refuses to pay the Pied Piper.

Pages 14 and 15
The Mayor tells the Pied Piper to 'do his worst'.

Pages 16 and 17
The Piper plays a tune and all the children follow him through a door which appears in the mountain.

Pages 18 and 19
One boy with a bad leg is left behind, but the other children and the Pied Piper are gone forever.

Pages 20 and 21
The town is a sad place with only memories of the children.

Robert Browning

- born in London in 1812
  - father worked at the Bank of England
  - started school at 8
  - began writing poetry at 14
  - went to London University
  - lived at home studying and writing until he was in his thirties
  - during the 1830s wrote plays and poetry and travelled to Italy and to Russia
- secretly married the poet Elizabeth Barrett in 1846
- lived in Italy with his wife and son, born in 1849
- with his wife, became well known as a writer
- his wife, Elizabeth Barrett Browning, died in 1861
- continued to write poetry and to travel
- died in Italy in 1889